CW00796197

a place to land

a place to land

a tanka prose memoir

Dru Philippou

Threadleaf Press

Printed by Kindle Direct Publishing

Cover Art: "Referring to Rembrandt (installation detail)"
by Betsy Kellas

Photographer: Liz Roozendaal

Cover Design: Douglas Fitch

ISBN: 9798743249398

Library of Congress Control Number: 2021914305

For Tulip, Lily, Daisy,
Willow, Simba, China, Zoe

Tell me the landscape in which you live,
and I will tell you who you are.

—José Ortega y Gasset

Contents

Foreword

A Place to Land

Goddesses

Gods

Communion

Foreword

The collection you're about to read consists entirely of tanka prose, a hybrid form with a history that dates back to ancient Japan. Its roots extend to the classic eighth-century Japanese poetry anthology *Man'yōshū* (*Collection of Ten Thousand Leaves*), where prefaces and headnotes are attached to five-line *waka* (forebear to the modern tanka). Its marriage of prose and poetry was elevated into art during Japan's Heian era (794 to 1185 A.D.), with the advent of diary literature (*nikki bungaku*) and poem tales (*uta monogatari*). In all cases, the tanka punctuated the prose with lyrical moments: an intimate window into the speaker's thoughts, a sudden epiphany, an insight inexpressible through prose alone.

Dru Philippou is among the best of today's writers who have chosen this form to tell her stories and memories. Together they compose a journey that raises a central question: what and where is home? They begin on the isle of Cyprus where she grew up on the cusp of that country's civil war between the Greek and Turkish Cypriots. She and her family moved to London when she was five, but the sights, sounds, and tastes of her native country remained with her—as captured in one of the book's first tanka:

> she seeks
> the myrtle's white bloom
> lily and crocus
> but demands most of all
> a red Cyprian rose

The first two sections in *A Place to Land* recount many of her memories from this time: the afternoons sharing coffee and sweets with a Turkish neighbor in Cyprus, before violence erupted; the echoes of those times in her new home in London, as her mother welcomed their fellow immigrants with "dishes of feta cheese, olives, pickled yellow peppers, hummus and pita for dipping." Several tanka prose pieces capture her alienation as she tries to fit into her new surroundings, the lure of her old language still strong as she tries to learn another tongue. They convey the influence of the women in her life (mother, grandmother) and the men (father, grandfather, uncle) who echo the "goddesses" and "gods" that populate many of these narratives. And throughout it all, like a recurring scent or song, the legacy of the author's native Cyprus, her Greek heritage. She plumbs the depths of her history and presents it anew.

> Making my way uphill to my childhood home, I catch
> a glimpse of the blue shutters folded like butterfly wings.
> The swing with its escape into sky. The barn where I
> hid when mother and father fought. I enter through
> the back door of the house using the key concealed
> among broken flowerpots, race through the half-dark
> hallway to my room. Dragging my toys from under the
> bed, I bring each plaything into the light.

> > orange-blossom air
> > wafts through a window . . .
> > I rock
> > my doll to sleep
> > with the old lullaby

> *from "Nostos"*

The third section of the book, "Communion," takes the reader into the author's current locale, New Mexico. The geography may be new, but the narratives again capture the spirit of her new region as well as its sights: horizons of mountain peaks, sand-blasted cabins overgrown with moss, desert bluebells, stagecoach trails, and the locals who populate this land of big horizons:

> Sugar's roadside barbecue joint, a tin-sided trailer,
> overlooks the Rio Grande. In the courtyard, apple
> trees shade picnic tables, a plastic owl poses on a
> stump, and lobelia spills over the sides of a wheel-
> barrow planter.

> A man wearing a chef's apron emerges from a plume
> of smoke and introduces himself as the owner. He
> points over his fence to the Old Spanish Trail that
> once opened the American Southwest to traders.

"I've been here seventeen years," he says. "There's nowhere else I want to be."

Read through this section, and it soon becomes clear that the chef's words could well be the author's. Through incisive and tender observations, the author makes clear that she has found a new home, has herself become grafted to its desert plains:

> a naked child
> casts her shadow
> in the sand
> sharp angles echo
> ancient petroglyphs

The book's epigraph quotes the Spanish philosopher José Ortega y Gasset: "Tell me the landscape in which you live, and I will tell you who you are." Part memoir, part spiritual pilgrimage, *A Place to Land* offers a glimpse into one woman's journey through the landscapes that make up her life, told through a marriage of prose and poetry, past and present. It's a personal but universal quest: the search for a place to land, for one's home, for one's self.

> the long road
> back home
> for the traveler
> the dream
> winds on forever

And now, it's time to begin . . .

— Rich Youmans
January 2022

A Place to Land

I follow
in the daubed footsteps
of a goddess
the rice paste
sticks to my feet

Whenever I feel as if I'm floating, I drive to Neem Karoli's ashram. In the temple room, I run my palm over the carpet, worn by bare or slippered feet. The air fills with incense and the harmonium's sustained note. A woman begins chanting, but I don't have the heart to join her. My attention wanders to the kitchen's clatter of stainless steel pans, to the brass ladle gurgling as someone dips it into the chai pot. A devotee sweeps, then slowly swishes a mop across the terra-cotta tiles.

Goddesses

Aphrodite

Curator Sophocles Hadjisavvas tells me the statue of Aphrodite, weathered by the sea, was found near Nea Paphos. Although she's missing her head, arms, and lower legs, her raised right arm may have held the ends of her long hair. Rivets, evidenced by rusty holes in her hips, once secured drapery to cover her legs.

> she seeks
> the myrtle's white bloom
> lily and crocus
> but demands most of all
> a red Cyprian rose

Kite Weather

Where is that perfect childhood when I dropped everything to
bike in the woods while dark was falling, with only the rhythm
of steady pedaling?

Where is that seaside town with its pink and lemon housefronts?
That warm air—a blend of caramel apples and cotton candy.
Where is that ruffled swimsuit every girl wears when bobbing
between waves, that handy bucket and spade for collecting
shells?

Where are those hours I spent idly, spoiled silly with dolls—
especially the one who differed from all the others, the one
with unruly hair and loose button eyes that I planted with
kisses. The one whose hand was worn from being held too
much, the one who grinned as if I had just told her a secret.

Where are those windy days that might billow a favorite
aunt's skirt and drag her off balance down the alley? Surely,
this weather is best for flying kites, when it feels like something
alive tugs at the end of the string.

> summers rich
> with stained fingers
> and easy laughter
> children picking
> blackberries
>
> all that vanishes
> into sea and sky
> beyond
> their careless tread
> across the harebells

ever farther
through a breach
of tangled hedge
the babbling brook
endlessly calling

Strovolos

What remains most vivid is our old Turkish neighbor as she calls my mother over for coffee and dessert: "Ela, kopiaste, ela." After coffee, she turns the small cups upside down on their saucers, waits for the grounds to settle. From behind her veil, she studies the dregs for my mother's future. I sit at a small table, pour sweetened black brew for my doll, and whisper my own fortune into her ear.

> white custard
> drenched in rosewater
> against the tide of terror
> what sweet things
> of life remain?

Later that year, I no longer hear the neighbor's welcome. Greek and Turkish Cypriots turn on each other, violence escalates to civil war.

Tug O' War

the island
disappears and reappears
floating in fog
my new home
evades discovery

The moment our ship docks in Southampton, we crowd to
the upper deck as officials step aboard. They instruct us in a
language we don't understand. An elderly woman, exhausted
by the voyage, sits on her suitcase and makes the sign of the
cross. Mom grabs one of my hands, Grandma the other; they
pull in opposite directions. I wrench free and slip into the shad-
ows, afraid to step ashore. Buttoning my wool coat against the
cold, I think of our chicken coop back home, an egg still warm
in my palm.

horns drown out
the screeching
of wind-battered gulls
the shouts of immigrants
clinging together

Holding On

grapevines weave
across the railings
of the front porch . . .
ancestors stare
in sepia tones

My mother welcomes other immigrants to her home in the new country with dishes of feta cheese, olives, pickled yellow peppers, hummus and pita for dipping. Greek coffee, or *Ellinikos kafes* as she calls it, is prepared in a copper pot and served in small white porcelain cups with matching saucers. As long as the women stay, coffee's available for each one's taste: *sketo, metrio, glyko*. Finally, she brings out glasses of water and the cherry spoon sweets. Hands brushing, everyone helps herself from the crystal bowl.

in the almond grove
behind her mother's house
she played with other kids,
counting and teasing
in colloquial Greek

The Corner Store

It stood at the end of our street and held everything a child could ever want. Sugar pigs with peach snouts. Rainbow dust and flying saucers. Jumbo gobstoppers and lollipops. I never could decide between licorice twists, kola kubes, fizzers, and boiled sweets sparkling like jewels. I loved the milk gums, four-for-a-penny. Best of all for a tenacious child like me was toffee—those long slow pulls with my teeth.

> clouding the glass
> with my breath
> I'm entranced
> by the *cha-ching*
> of the cash register

> my halfpenny
> rolls under the counter
> far from reach
> the jar thuds
> back into place

First Day

the schoolyard gate
swings inward—
hand-in-hand
mother and daughter enter
under the skittish clouds

A brass bell rings nine times—an autumn morning, 1967. I
step over the threshold and up the stairway in my bottle-green
uniform. I tighten my red sash and tie and, barely able to
breathe, slowly turn the classroom doorknob. Attendance
taken, Bibles in hand, we walk in single file to the main hall
for prayers and hymns.

In the afternoon, I learn to wrap books in brown paper for
protection. I also learn names: Miss Henn, Headmistress; Miss
Winter, Form teacher; Miss Cross, Religion; and others such as
Mrs. Moon, Miss Popple, and Mrs. Sugar.

days later
my Italian friend Anna
giggles at the names,
waving blouse sleeves
longer than her arms

Until We Speak English

A classmate stands alone in the school playground, a doll under her arm.

>faded ribbons
>in long black hair,
>tiny feet
>half-hidden by her skirt . . .
>eyes glassy and wide open

She lifts the doll and holds her close to the wire fence so she can look out, too. I leave my bench and walk toward them. The girl utters a few words in her language and I in mine, no shared words between us. The doll just stares.

Imago

We teenagers sit in a circle making aprons. As we work, our teacher tells stories of ancestors binding skin with bone, wood, and ivory; of Mary Queen of Scots in the Tower, whiling away her time with needlework. The Scotch thistle, Tudor rose, and French lily were some of her motifs.

I watch Cynthia's nimble fingers weave a needle in and out along the stenciled line, her rose appliqué held by a safety pin. Chloris unpicks another crooked line; a drop of blood beads. I moisten my lips and twist the strand, wink at the glint of silver. Pulling my fabric taut, I poke the ruffled hem of my knee-length apron. I pin a heart-shaped pocket like Grandma's. Trying the apron on for size, I tie the long strings in front and run my palm down its length. I cut loose threads from the back.

> wings embroidered
> in red and magenta
> blue and gold
> a butterfly lifts
> off the wild plum

Odder and Taller

How long have I stood by this window? My yard is empty
except for the potted four o'clocks on the railroad-tie steps.
Now I stare, as I often do, above their crimson heads, through
the gate, down the lane, all the way back to Sasha's birthday
party . . .

The invitation said "fancy hats." On a large piece of paper, I
painted the ocean with fish tailing away into the blue. Green
tissue, crumpled in my hands, became seaweed. I glued the
paper edges together to form a cylinder hat. From the shelf,
I grabbed one of Papa's paper boats made out of newspaper.
I wrote BREEZE across the sail and placed the boat gently
on the waves.

In a game of ring toss, I felt my hat towering far above the
other children's. I hurled the ring toward the peg, watched
as it glided over the snickering kids and found its home.

> long summer day
> on the hazy pond
> a paper boat angles
> as though it will sail
> right to my hands

Pool of Dreams

Each summer of my childhood, I went down through the woods
to a hidden pond. I took off my shoes, slipped into the limpid
water and breaststroked for hours, past the white lilies, under
a day moon, then onward with a backstroke. Sometimes I sank
to test the pebbly bottom with my feet. Sometimes I rested,
floating on my back, letting the ruffled water caress my face.
Eventually, I climbed out onto a boulder in the waning light
to sit and listen.

    the rattle
    of a hand-painted pod
    this treasure
    stashed between rocks
    reawakens a child's rhyme

    glinting
    in autumn's evening light
    a shoe buckle
    half-buried in the ground—
    what journeys it has seen

At Closing

A crystal chandelier sheds glittering light over the "sold" ivory
wing chair. I rummage through a box of lace doilies and table-
runners by the hushed aisle of books. Handbags and hats are
up for grabs. Ball gowns. An array of vintage dresses. Nothing
so far soothes. In the bric-a-brac, I find a tea cosy like my
Grandma's and bury it under the pile.

> beyond
> the child's fingertips
> weighted with longing
> a heart-shaped stone
> hangs from a ribbon

Gods

Nostos

memories
wash up like seaweed
on distant shores
who will untangle
yesterday from today

Making my way uphill to my childhood home, I catch a glimpse
of the blue shutters folded like butterfly wings. The swing with
its escape into sky. The barn where I hid when mother and
father fought. I enter through the back door of the house using
the key concealed among broken flowerpots, race through the
half-dark hallway to my room. Dragging my toys from under
the bed, I bring each plaything into the light.

orange-blossom air
wafts through a window . . .
I rock
my doll to sleep
with the old lullaby

I step into the garden, close my eyes, and catch whispers of
the past borne on Zephyrus' breath. After years of absence
from my birthplace, I feel like another intruder. Successive
waves of invaders have colonized this island at the crossroads
of continents. For nearly half a century, it has been divided in
two by the Green Line.

a solano bush,
brutally cut back
by a neighbor,
leans against
a rust-eaten fence

Independence Day, 1960

After gathering grapes all morning, Grandpa heads for shade near his ivy-crowned statue of Dionysus. He places a cluster of grapes at the god's feet and praises him for viticulture. Sitting down on a stump, he spreads his lunch of bread, halloumi, olives, and tomatoes on a checkered napkin. He pours sweet wine into his bowl and drinks to the rousing chorus of cicadas, to the ripening glow of harvest.

> a long climb
> up the vineyard terrace
> where a furrow holds its flag—
> green, copper, and white
> in the wind

Warriors

visions gather
and take the shape
of a long oar—
one warrior's shadow
slides across the strand

Grivas, striving
for the ideal of *enosis*,
tosses his army cap
into the blinding sun,
into a new era

His *nom de guerre* is that of the Byzantine hero, Digenis
Akritas, who guarded the borders of Cyprus and chased
away Saracen pirates.

Neither Seen nor Heard

Cattle kick up dust along the dirt road that runs past our house. I'm three years old and drawn to a cow with large brown eyes, long lashes. I step off the porch and chase after her. Her warm breath feels soft on my cheek; her calf nuzzles her belly. We wander into an orange orchard. I'm plucking grass for them when the herder arrives with his stick. He guides his livestock back through the gate, with me hidden in their midst.

> a curfew siren
> louder than cowbells—
> my father lifts me
> from the herd
> to the safety of home

Caramanian Mountains

My father once told me a tale about a plague of locusts. He saw them early one morning looming on the horizon—a churning black cloud from the direction of the Karpaz Peninsula, where the fair people lived in carved stone houses. The insects landed on father's artichoke bushes and devoured them to the roots. They laid waste to the thyme mother loved to crush between her fingers. When the sky filled again with their rustling, wild donkeys brayed, rousing partridges from the undergrowth. The swarm settled into a neighboring farmer's cornfield and then the winds of Asia Minor carried them west.

> so close
> almost within reach
> of my voice
> these legendary heights
> shed their shadows

I repeated this story to my school friends, wanting to believe it really happened. I lingered over the word *Caramanian* because it sounded exotic. I told them other stories, too, as if my father had a huge presence in my life.

Holy Fire

As I join the crowd of children surrounding the knife-grinder,
Mrs. Walder struggles down her steps, carrying a bundle of
knives wrapped in muslin. I run to fetch them for the grinder.
He adjusts his spectacles, pumps his bicycle pedals. Pressing
a bone-handled carving knife to the spinning grindstone, he
whisks it back and forth, running his thumb along the edge,
testing the blade's sharpness. He grabs another knife and the
heavenly whir begins again. Golden sparks fly into our faces,
but no one dares surrender their place.

> knives and scissors
> shears and daggers
> objects of mastery
> this mender
> of children's hearts

Our God's Green Staff

enshrined forever
in Delos, in Delphi
and in Thebes—
Dionysus in the slumber
of a summer day

My best friend Jill and I skip class and head for the mountain
hot springs. Lips stained with red wine from our fathers' cabi-
nets, we splash each other and laugh, sharing old stories
through a long afternoon. Slowly we climb out of the water
onto a bed of blue-green grass. The clatter of hooves echoes
as dreamlike figures pass. We follow them over meadows and
through pine groves but cannot keep up.

potted ivy
twines through words
in chalk . . .
the startling clamor
of the classroom bell

White Space

When my father lost his job of twenty years, I hoped to
get to know him better. I yearned to hear stories about his
parents, how he met my mother, and what his village in
Cyprus was like during British rule. But most of the time,
he sat in front of the TV drinking whisky and clouding the
room with cigarette smoke.

One afternoon, with a sudden burst of energy, he removed
all the living room furniture and began re-decorating.

>a light touch
>makes the paint last longer—
>the smile
>I'd known in childhood
>whitewashed in sadness

He worked rapidly, never saying a word, occasionally stirring
the paint. When he finished, he glanced around the room.
Where the portrait of his mother had once hung, a nail hole
patched with spackle.

>white space
>in Japanese painting
>lays bare
>some small object
>in a corner

Sanctum

wild bursts
of poppies
open to the heavens—
the temple of Apollo
with its guardian lions

I run a red crayon over Uncle's free-floating columns drawn
on paper, shading the emptiness between them green. With
a pencil, I taper each column with shallow flutes, setting them
onto stylobates. I sketch the abacuses and place them on capi-
tals. Standing back, I gaze at the towering pillars, imagine them
bearing loads. I reach for another pencil, thicken the walls
around me, and slowly tilt back my head.

Immortal

these heights
that summer's humidity
cannot reach—
Paphos Blue butterflies
flying free

The mountain village of Tsada overlooks a bay. I make my way
through the garden of a small Byzantine monastery. A hermit
monk shows me the church's single icon and its bell tower, then
we sit on a bench under the arches and he tells me the story of
Evagoras, teenage poet, born in this village. Fighting for liberty
in 1957, he was caught with a gun and sent to the British gallows
of Nicosia. The monk points me toward Tsada's two-domed
church, *Panayia Chryseleaousas*. A statue of Evagoras and the
Heroes Monument stand out of sight beyond it. Before I leave,
the monk reaches for my hand and recites some verses by the
poet.

I'll take a road uphill
I'll take the paths
To find the stairs
That lead to freedom

Searching for freedom
I'll have as company
The white snow
Mountains and torrents

Communion

Hipólito, the Herder (1912-1971)

with his crook
he navigates
the rough terrain
early bluegrass
and white clover

villagers
liken the shepherd
to ruddy-limbed Pan
piping to nymphs
near a spring

rustic viands
for his fare
and tinkling bells
the heavenly sleep
of the herder

My friend tells me: "Go down from the trail over the matted
grass and up along the fence. Pass the water trough to the cedar
in the distance, shading the grave and the red and yellow tulips
that I planted last year. Hipólito is buried there." Nothing but
his birth and death are known, chiseled in a wooden cross. But
my friend often says, "Go by Hipólito's grave."

Passing By

I hike down a four-hundred-foot drop, an old stagecoach trail,
to the hot springs along the Rio Grande where travelers stopped
to rest. Though the cluster of cabins was destroyed by a flood
in 1927, remnants of the bridge are still embedded in concrete.
Here women once gathered at the pools to bathe and wash
clothes. Long before the Spanish arrived, Native Americans
called these springs *Wa-pu-mee*, waters of long life.

> a naked child
> casts her shadow
> in the sand
> sharp angles echo
> ancient petroglyphs
>
> in a hundred years
> who will see my imprint
> who will know
> I knelt at the edge
> of this river

Holiday Paradise

on the hillside
a prospecting hole
the tailings'
magical glitter
of fool's gold

On this Labor Day weekend, bikers speed up a rutted road that dead-ends at the Cabresto Lake Campground. In the back of a truck, children in goggles shield their eyes from the dust while checking cell phones. Their grandma is seated in the front seat. Her candy-pink fingernails gleam through a small dog's white fur. At a curve overlooking Hell's Canyon, a scrap of silver foil floats over the precipice. The driver slows down. A man in flip-flops is struggling to replace a ruptured tire on his Northstar pop-up camper. Behind, an overweight man on an ATV yells at him to let him through.

awakened
by radio crackles
a camper
discovers a night
of falling stars

Last Outpost

Sugar's roadside barbecue joint, a tin-sided trailer, overlooks the Rio Grande. In the courtyard, apple trees shade picnic tables, a plastic owl poses on a stump, and lobelia spills over the edge of a wheelbarrow planter.

A man wearing a chef's apron emerges from a plume of smoke and introduces himself as the owner. He points over his fence to the Old Spanish Trail that once opened the American Southwest to traders. "I've been here seventeen years," he says. "There's nowhere else I want to be."

A bone-shaped headstone bears the name of his beloved bull-dog, Sugar. I sit at my table and watch motorists ordering take-out.

> the long road
> back home
> for the traveler
> the dream
> winds on forever

From Water to Land

My blue kayak glides through Eagle Nest Lake to a narrow
channel that leads to a dam, one hundred and forty feet high.
I steer over the floating rope barrier, then past *Do Not Go
Beyond This Point*. After securing my boat, I step onto the
bank, noonday sunshine at my back. I sway with an unsteady
gait, remnant swells still in my limbs. On all fours, I climb the
slope and then the metal staircase, quickly walk the dam from
end to end, noticing long, sinuous cracks in the concrete.

Going down, I dislodge a rock that seems to roll toward the
edge forever.

> a tetrapod
> joins its shadow
> on the shore
> lapping waves
> beckon it back

Old Friends

A volunteer grows among my cucumber vines. Heart-shaped
leaves, borne on petioles, seem unfamiliar. The silvery-haired
stems have a fuzzy feel. I circle the newcomer with stones,
provide plenty of water, and check it several times a day.
Chalice-like blooms emerge, luminous blue.

> behind me
> mountains rise
> silent and shadowed
> their small secrets
> tucked away

Slowly, a memory arises from my years of wilderness hiking:
mountain bluebell, harebell, common bluebell . . . my unexpect-
ed visitor is a desert bluebell, *Phacelia campanularia*, native to
California and the arid southwest.

> you kept me company
> when I roamed
> the haunts
> of every flower . . .
> again, I call your name

No Vacancy

Sand blows against the panes of a deserted house, blasting them
opaque. Jacks keep the building from collapsing; metal columns
support an upper deck. The staircase caved in long ago. I lean
against a beam that's twisted out of its foundation. Someone has
spray-painted red flowers on the walls, and a giant notice board
warns DANGER. Broken floorboards reveal a carpet of moss,
and a hole in the roof admits the sky.

> one endless day
> after another . . .
> birdsong
> fills the space
> you left behind

End of Summer

I will hike up Lobo Peak through San Cristobal Canyon until the light is gone and I am no more than a part of the night. I could venture halfway to the meadow, but today I want to soar into the alpine air, sit alone, and smooth the wrinkled pages of my book.

all is faded now
moored gently
to this earth
a purple-blue gentian
nudges the breeze

Sloughing Off

what blooms
and bones she keeps
they are props
that she will paint
beside her mountain

I see myself climbing Cerro Pedernal, bounding up the butte
in no time. At the top, where Georgia O'Keeffe's ashes were
scattered, I could race along the narrow ridge in the wind's
handclasp, plunge headlong into the blue, slough off my skin
among pink hollyhocks, return home as a stranger.

"Road in Maine"

At any moment, I expect to see sunlight ruffled by ocean, a trawler bringing the day's catch to shore, children in bright swimsuits launching paper boats by the water's edge.

But broad daylight falls silently on beach plums, heavy with clusters of ripened fruit. The wing print of a gull vanishes into the sky.

I cannot remember how far I drove before turning back. The road ran forever and went nowhere. When I return, I cannot find it again.

> I wear the brooch
> my mother wore—
> unspoken words
> like tumbled shells
> lie along the shore

Even when I describe the wireless telephone poles, no one can point the way.

"First Naiveté"

The latest young recruit at the ashram is seated on the hallway floor practicing tabla. Inside the temple room, another man, robed in saffron and a bright lemon wool hat, gives praise to Durga. Someone else is chanting. Evening aarti begins and a pujari calls out the deities.

> on the altar
> flowers always flowers
> so vibrant
> they seem unreal
> until I touch them

Notes

"Strovolos": "Ela, kopiaste, ela" translates as "Come and share my food, come."

"Holding On": "*sketo, metrio, glyko*" translates as "unsweetened, medium sweet, sweet."

"Warriors": General Georgios Grivas, led the National Organization of Cypriot Struggle or EOKA, a guerrilla group that fought for *enosis* (union with Greece) and to end British rule.

"Immortal": Evagoras Pallikarides (1938-1957) was a member of EOKA. He was executed by the British at nineteen years of age.

"'Road in Maine'": painting by Edward Hopper (1914). See https://www.edwardhopper.net/road-in-maine.jsp

"'First Naiveté'": This is a concept developed by the French philosopher Paul Ricoeur that outlines our naïve understanding of things, first perceiving them without judgment, then in a more critical way. He also describes a "second naiveté" that exists beyond the realm of criticism.

Acknowledgments

My sincere thanks to the editors of the following journals where these works first appeared in slightly different versions: *Contemporary Haibun Online, Drifting Sands, Haibun Today, Modern English Tanka, Modern Haibun and Tanka Prose,* and *Ribbons.*

I'm deeply grateful to Jenny Ward Angyal, Autumn Noelle Hall, Jeffrey Woodward, and Rich Youmans for their careful reading of the manuscript and thoughtful comments.

About the Author

Dru Philippou was born on the island of Cyprus and lived there until the age of five. Her family then moved to London, where she was raised. She received her M.F.A. in Creative Writing from Naropa University in Colorado and now lives in northern New Mexico. An award-winning poet, she has received two Pushcart Prize nominations for her poetry, which has been widely published and anthologized. In her spare time, she hikes and backpacks the wilderness areas near her home, which nourish both her spirit and her writing.

Printed in Great Britain
by Amazon

84854050R00048